The
Bike Challenge

Patrick Morgan

Learning Media

Contents

1. The Challenge

Myra's heart is pumping hard as she stands on the start line. She's one of more than six hundred bikers getting set to face one of the world's toughest mountain bike events. Myra's nervous. What if she can't make the climbs or crashes on the downhills? But she knows that she's put the work in. She's trained hard for five weeks for this. She's ready for the challenge.

Myra Moller started biking when she was five, riding with her family. She took up mountain bike racing at twelve and did well in local races. Now, at sixteen, Myra competes in national and international events.

"I love riding fast, with the wind whistling through my helmet. It's great, feeling my heart beat hard as I climb a steep hill. Mountain biking is awesome!"

As well as mountain biking, Myra likes cross-country running and soccer. She's also tried hockey, springboard diving, and **tae kwon do**.

"I love competing in lots of sports, but mountain biking is my favorite."

This year, Myra's decided to take up one of the mountain biker's greatest challenges: the Karapoti Classic. It's a tough, 30-mile race through dense forest. She'll be riding for more than three hours, over rocks, streams, and mud and up and down huge hills. Sounds great!

2. The Equipment

The Bike

Myra's bike is specially designed for cross-country racing.

• suspension forks that absorb bumps to make riding smoother and easier
• powerful **V-brakes**
• drink bottle holder to carry water for long rides
• clip-in pedals to stop Myra's feet from slipping off the pedals and to help her pedal strongly
• knobby tires for grip

• safety helmet to protect Myra's head if she falls off

The Clothes

Myra wears special clothes when she rides. They fit snugly so that they won't catch on bushes or flap in the wind. She wears a helmet, gloves, and sunglasses for protection.

• padded shorts to make longer rides more comfortable

• shoes that clip onto the pedals

- sunglasses to protect Myra's eyes from sun, dust, mud, and bugs

- fingerless gloves to give Myra better grip on the handlebars and to protect her hands

- a snug, colorful jersey that has pockets on the back for food and displays the name of her **sponsor**

From Beach Cruiser to Mountain Bike

Mountain biking began in California in the 1970s when a group of friends began riding old beach cruiser bikes down rough tracks on big hills. These bikes were heavy and, without gears, were no good for riding uphill. They often fell apart under the strain. So inventors added gears, better brakes, and lightweight frames. The mountain bike was born.

Today, mountain bikers ride everywhere – on beaches, dirt roads, mountain trails, and city streets. They even compete at the Olympic Games.

An Early Mountain Bike

- heavy steel frame from an old beach cruiser bike
- straight forks, no suspension
- fat tires
- 15-speed gears
- hub brakes with brake levers recycled from a motorbike.

3. Training

Five weeks before the race, Myra begins training six days a week. To take up the Karapoti challenge, Myra knows she will need:

- ***endurance*** to ride for up to four hours;
- *strength* to climb three steep hills; and
- *skill* to ride over rocks, roots, and ruts.

To improve her endurance, she goes for long rides on the weekends. Each weekend, she adds an hour to her rides to get used to biking for up to four hours. In the two weeks before race day, she shortens the rides so that she won't be too tired to race. This is called "tapering."

To build up her strength, Myra does a lot of hill biking. She rides up bigger and bigger hills as the weeks go by. She also swims and lifts weights at the gym. Myra's lucky – her dad runs a gym and helps Myra to plan her strength training.

"Lifting weights has improved my strength. Now I can carry my bike up the steepest hills and lift it over a fence by myself."

To practice her biking skills, Myra rides over "technical" tracks. These have lots of obstacles, such as loose rocks, muddy puddles, slippery dirt, and gnarly **drop-offs**. To keep the bike gripping on steep climbs, she sits forward on the saddle and relaxes her upper body.

As well as all this exercise, Myra has a rest day once a week. This helps her body to recover from her tough training schedule and stay in top shape for racing.

<table>
<tr><th></th><th>Week 1</th><th>Week 2</th><th>Week 3</th><th>Week 4</th><th>Week 5</th></tr>
<tr><th>Monday</th><td>30 minutes: gym</td><td colspan="4">1 hour: gym</td></tr>
<tr><th>Tuesday</th><td>1 hour: easy ride</td><td>2 hours: ride over medium hills</td><td>2 hours: ride over big hills</td><td>2 hours: ride over big hills</td><td>1 hour: ride over medium hills</td></tr>
<tr><th rowspan="2">Wednesday</th><td>30 minutes: gym</td><td colspan="4">1 hour: gym</td></tr>
<tr><td colspan="5">40 minutes: squash, 80 minutes: soccer</td></tr>
<tr><th>Thursday</th><td>1 hour: easy ride</td><td>2 hours: easy ride</td><td>3 hours: easy ride</td><td>2 hours: easy ride</td><td>1 hour: easy ride</td></tr>
<tr><th>Friday</th><td colspan="5">rest day, 20 minutes: run</td></tr>
<tr><th>Saturday</th><td>2 hours: easy ride</td><td>1 hour: easy ride</td><td>2 hours: easy ride</td><td>2 hours: easy ride</td><td>1 hour: easy ride over the race course</td></tr>
<tr><th>Sunday</th><td>2 hours: ride over big hills</td><td>3 hours: race</td><td>4 hours: ride over the race course</td><td>2 hours: ride over big hills</td><td>Race day</td></tr>
</table>

Diet

Myra needs plenty of food to give her enough energy to train and race. She makes sure she eats a lot of **carbohydrates**, such as cereal, toast, and beans.

"I get really hungry. I eat heaps after hard exercise."

She drinks special milkshakes that contain calcium (for her bones) and vitamins (to help to prevent illness).

On long rides, Myra sips water from a bottle in her backpack or mounted on her bike. She carries fruit, chocolate, and energy bars in the back pocket of her jersey to eat along the way.

4. Race Day

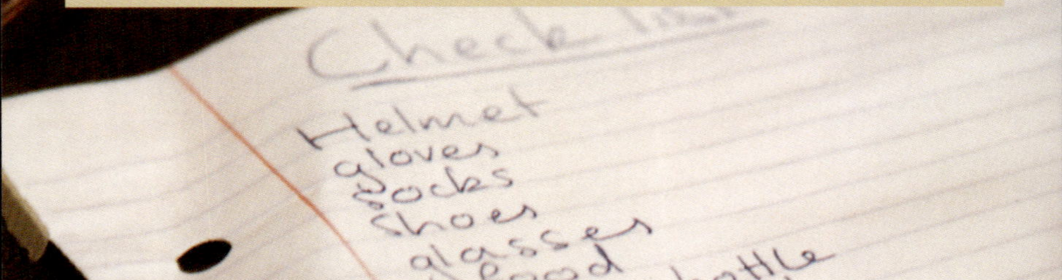

It's race day at last and an early start for Myra and her family to get to the race venue on time. Myra's excitement grows when she sees all the other bikers buzzing around the car park like colorful insects. This is it! She's done her training. There's nothing left to do now but just go for it.

At the Start Line

There are way too many bikers for everyone to start at the same time. So they are grouped by their age and whether they are male or female. The fastest groups start first. There aren't many girls racing today, so Myra's starting with a group of women riders.

The starting horn blares. Myra lifts her bike onto her shoulder and runs toward the first obstacle – the river. It's not deep, but the water is cold as it soaks through her shoes and socks. No time to worry about that. The riders are all splashing across and out onto the start of the track. Myra mounts her bike and gets going as fast as she can. She picks a gear that allows her to pedal steadily and tries to keep up with the riders around her.

Climbing

Myra's breathing hard as she races up the first hill. She can hear the scrunch of her tires on the gravel. It seems to take forever to climb the steep track. At last she reaches the summit of the hill, and then she's over the top.

Downhill

The dirt track here is slippery, so Myra's careful not to brake too hard. She doesn't want to skid off the track into the bushes or over a cliff.

Myra likes going really fast. She tries to catch up with the riders she can see ahead. It gets steep and rocky, so she slides off the back of the saddle and balances above the back wheel. The bike's suspension forks absorb the bumps. Myra relaxes her legs and hangs on tight. On the way, she passes some people who are walking their bikes down.

"I used to be scared on rough downhills, too, but now that I've had lots of practice, I can go really fast without crashing. It's fun!"

Myra's been drinking plenty of water from her backpack. After riding for an hour, she feels hungry as well as thirsty. She reaches into her back pocket for a chocolate bar and opens it with her teeth. She's feeling good, going well, then ….

Puncture

Pssstt! Myra hits a rock, hard, and all the air rushes out of her tire. A puncture! As quick as she can, she removes the wheel, pulls the tire off, and looks for the hole in the tube. It's a snakebite puncture – two slits. There's no time to patch it. She pulls a spare tube from her toolbag, fits it to the tire, and pumps it up. As she's putting the wheel back on, some riders pass and call out a few words of encouragement. She grins and waves to them, and soon she's pedaling hard again.

Mud

Two hours have gone now. The track gets really muddy. Myra's sunglasses keep the sludgy water from getting into her eyes. Sometimes the mud is too deep to ride through, and her bike squelches to a halt. Then she has to jump off and carry her bike. She's covered in mud, but it's kind of fun being so messy.

The ground gets firmer, and she's riding again. Her time is looking OK, but that's no reason to ease off. Gotta keep pushing the pace!

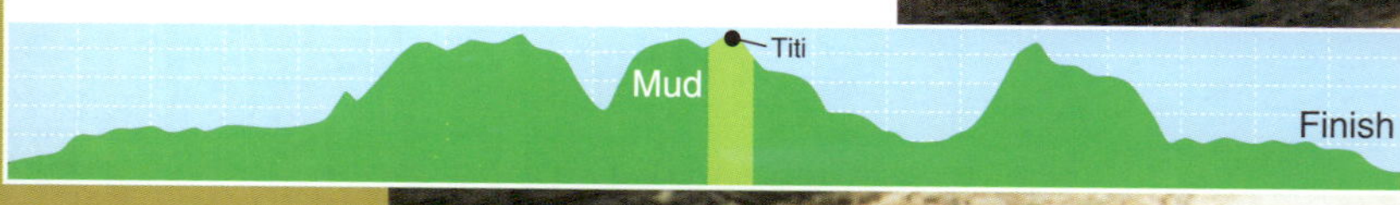

Finish

One last, long downhill, and then she knows that she's getting near the end. Myra's legs are really tired, but she can see the crowd at the finish line now. They are shouting to her to keep going, so she makes a final effort. She splashes back across the river, and then she's pedaling across the finish line. People clap and cheer, and some call out her name. Myra checks her watch: 3 hours 28 minutes. That's an even better time than she'd hoped for!

“I’m aching all over – my face is caked in sweat and grime – but I feel great. I did it! I met the mountain bike challenge!”

Titi (2,010 feet)
Deadwood (1,885 feet)
Dopers (1,740 feet)
Start/ finish line
Karapoti Gorge
The Karapoti Classic Race Course
Karapoti Race Track
Rivers/streams
Road
Hilly areas
Direction of race

Glossary

(These words are printed in bold type the first time they appear in the book.)

aluminum alloy: aluminum that has been strengthened with other metals

carbohydrates: energy foods like bread, cereal, cookies, rice, pasta, and starchy vegetables such as potatoes and corn

drop-off: a big step down

endurance: to be able to keep going for a long time

gears: the system of cogs that makes the pedals turn the back wheel at different speeds

sponsor: a person or company that provides support and money

tae kwon do: a Korean martial art

V-brakes: high-performance mountain bike brakes